ELLIS ISLAND

CAROL M. HIGHSMITH AND TED LANDPHAIR

CRESCENT BOOKS

NEW YORK

This 2000 edition is published by
Crescent Books®, an imprint of Random House Value Publishing, Inc.,
201 East 50th Street, New York, N.Y. 10022.

Crescent Books® and colophon are registered trademarks of
Random House Value Publishing, Inc.

Random House
New York • Toronto • London • Sydney • Auckland
http://www.randomhouse.com/

Printed and bound in China

Library of Congress Cataloging-in-Publication Data
Highsmith, Carol M., 1946–
Ellis Island / Carol M. Highsmith and Ted Landphair.
p. cm.
ISBN 0-517-20879-2
1. Ellis Island Immigration Station (N.Y. and N.J.)—History Pictorial works.
2. Immigrants—United States—History Pictorial works.
3. Ellis Island (N.J. and N.Y.)—Pictorial works.
4. United States—Emigration and immigration—History Pictorial works.
I. Landphair, Ted, 1942– . II. Title.
JV6484.H54 2000   99–27774
974.7'1—dc21   CIP

8   7   6   5   4   3   2   1

Project Editor: Donna Lee Lurker
Designed by Robert L. Wiser, Archetype Press, Inc., Washington, D.C.

All photographs by Carol M. Highsmith unless otherwise credited:
Ellis Island National Monument Library, pp. 8–9, 16, 18, 26–29, 38, 40–41, 44, 46, 49, 54, 56, 58;
Mystic Seaport Museum, Mystic, Connecticut, p. 19; Augustus Sherman/Ellis Island National
Monument Library, pp. 36–37, 39; Smithsonian National Museum of American History, p. 60.

*The authors wish to thank the following for their generous assistance
in connection with the completion of this book:*

Frank Mills, Deputy Superintendent; and Toni Best, Administrative Assistant,
Statue of Liberty/Ellis Island National Monument

Elizabeth Carroll, National Park Service Interpretive Guide

Ellis Island Security Staff

FOREWORD

One-third of Americans have something in common. At least one of their ancestors immigrated to the United States through teeming Ellis Island in New York Harbor. More than twelve million people passed through this complex from 1892 until it closed in 1954. Restrictive immigration acts passed in 1924 reduced the flood to a trickle, and Ellis was largely converted into a Coast Guard station and wartime detention center before it was shuttered and left to molder. But in the 1980s a $315 million restoration project—the most ambitious in U.S. history—refurbished Ellis Island's Main Building as well as the nearby Statue of Liberty. Close to six million visitors annually now ferry from Manhattan or New Jersey to Liberty Island. About one-third go on to Ellis Island.

In 1882 the Federal Government, worried about the spread of dreaded diseases like typhoid fever, took control of the immigration process from the states. It set up stations in places like New Orleans, Angel Island in San Francisco Bay, and Castle Garden, an old fort in Manhattan's Battery Park. As the crush of newcomers overwhelmed Castle Garden, the Immigration Bureau commissioned a gigantic processing center on a four-acre island once owned by New Yorker Samuel Ellis. Using subway rubble and ships' ballast, engineers quadrupled the size of the island. But the wooden immigration center burned to the ground in 1897. Ornate, red-brick and white-limestone replacement structures—including a magnificent main building with four cupola towers—opened on December 17, 1900.

Ellis Island became a polyglot city on three islands linked by a ferry dock. Hospitals, quarantine buildings, and detention centers rose on unnamed Islands Two and Three. Decrepit today, they stand empty in heaps of fallen plaster.

When steamships entered New York Harbor, immigration inspectors sailed out for a perfunctory check of the paperwork of first- and second-class passengers. Steerage passengers were sent to Ellis Island for close scrutiny. Five thousand immigrants a day—the record was 11,747 on April 7, 1907—were sorted into lots of 250. Anyone over two years old was required to walk unaided up stairs to the mammoth Registry Room, where physicians looking for contagious diseases and emotional impairments administered a "thirty-second medical" exam. The immigrants were chalked with a code and shunted into more lines, often for hours, before being questioned about their paperwork, criminal records, and work status.

Ultimately immigrants were funneled down the "Stairs of Separation," divided into three sections. Those descending on the right proceeded to a New Jersey train station; those on the left caught a ferry to Manhattan's squalid tenement district. The center section was reserved for detainees bound for legal hearings, hospitalization, or deportation. While Ellis Island has been called the "Isle of Tears," about 97 per cent of arriving immigrants were eventually approved for admission.

Ellis's processing center reopened in 1990 as the National Park Service's immigrant museum. Galleries are packed with haunting photographs as well as religious icons, household goods, and humble valises—often representing the sum total of an immigrant's possessions. Outside is a curving, stainless-steel Wall of Honor into which more than five hundred thousand names have been etched as a memorial gift from immigrants' descendants. The visitor experience can be profound. With Lady Liberty towering across the harbor, Ellis Island stands as a monument to the "golden door" beyond which "huddled masses yearning to breathe free" undertook a new life.

FRONT COVER: Ellis Island's processing center, hospitals, and quarantine buildings, directly across the Hudson River from lower Manhattan, were the doorway to America for hundreds of thousands of immigrants. BACK COVER: The multi-ethnic faces of America appear among the stars and stripes of an exhibit by Pablo Delano. PAGE 1: Jeanne Rynhart's Emigrant Statue of Annie Moore and her brothers stands on the wharf in Cobh, Ireland. They were the first to arrive at Ellis Island in 1892. PAGES 2–3: Immigrants deemed medically or legally unfit were detained in now-deteriorated buildings.

1906

ALLAN LINE

HANDBOOK

Every INTENDING EMIGRANT to CANADA OR THE UNITED STATES SHOULD READ THIS BOOK.

Kommando-Brücke.

Sonnendeck. Grillroom. Passag.-Kammer I Cl. Sonnendec

Promenadendeck. Rauchsalon I Cl. Gesellschaftssalon.Promenadende

Gang. Post-Bureau. Gang. Luxus-Cabine.

Speise-Salon I Classe.

Passag. II Cl. Küche f. Zwischendeck. Speise- u.Schlafraum f. Zwischendecker. Barbier.

Schlachterei. Gang. Fleisch. Proviant-Raum. Obst. Gang. Gepäck.

Kohlen. Ladung. Ladung. Ladung. Kohlen.

Übersicht
der Innenräume des Doppelschrauben-Schnellpoftdampfers
«Deutſchland».

The Allan Line was one of many steamship companies that accepted emigrants. Its handbook (opposite) notes that well-to-do English passengers need fear no examination before crossing the Atlantic. Indeed first- and second-class travelers avoided Ellis Island as well. The Hamburg-America Line's brochure for 1906 (left) featured a cutaway view of the SS *Deutschland* that showed the crowded steerage section, called the *Zwischendeck*. It held 280 passengers who slept on closely stacked bunks.

Immigrants arriving at New York Harbor understandably crowded on deck (left) to get a glimpse of their anticipated new homeland. Actually their first sight of America came off Montauk Point, Long Island, where a lighthouse tower was visible for miles. Just about every immigrant knew the inspirational meaning of the Statue of Liberty (above), which was passed just before landing at Battery Point in Manhattan. Steerage passengers were then ferried to Ellis Island.

Liberty Island (above) is still an exhilarating sight. Ellis Island is directly behind Lady Liberty; Jersey City, New Jersey, to the left; and Manhattan in the distance to the right. A bust of Statue of Liberty sculptor Auguste Bartholdi (opposite) was a gift to the Ellis Island library from the Bartholdi Museum in Colmar, France. The deterioration of structures on Ellis's Islands Two and Three, in the foreground (overleaf) is not so apparent from the air.

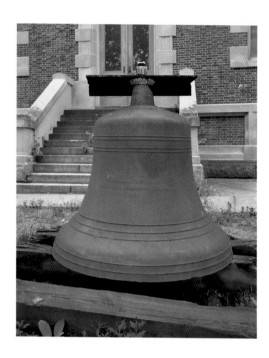

The U.S. Immigration Service hung this giant 1905 ship's bell (above) in the Ellis Island harbor. Ferries full of immigrants from Battery Park in New York arrived at this landing and debarkation building (right), which has not yet been restored. Its passageways connect Ellis's main island with Islands Two and Three, which were largely man-made from New York City subway rubble and ships' ballast—often from the very steamships that carried immigrants to America.

Immigrants off-load at Ellis Island (top right). Note their manifest tags—an example of which appears below (bottom right). These tags were issued by steamship lines whose screening process was almost as rigorous as those at Ellis. That is because the companies were required to pay for the passage home of any of their immigrant passengers rejected for admission to the United States. The immigrant experience was captured on a 1998 U.S. postage stamp (opposite).

S.S. .... "NEW YORK"
From LIVERPOOL, ...23rd January, 1915....

MANIFEST SHEET No.

3

NAME.

Albert Bertha

LIST No. 13   See Back.

Two women from Guadeloupe (above) arrive at Ellis Island in 1911. In the first part of the twentieth century, ferries (right) did not carry tourists to Ellis Island. They were the immigrants' link to Ellis from the steamships that had brought them to America. A firm headed by John Belle— himself an immigrant from Wales—rehabilitated Ellis Island's main processing center (overleaf) in the 1980s as part of the most ambitious restoration project in American history.

Ellis Island's immigration station officially opened in 1892, but most of its wooden buildings burned to the ground in a devastating fire five years later. Boring & Tilton, a small New York architectural firm, designed sturdier brick and limestone replacements. The firm was one of the first outside contractors to complete federal government buildings. It submitted a massive, highly ornamented design with elaborate details like arched entryways (opposite), sculpted statuary (left), and trademark cupola towers (above).

The entire first floor of Ellis Island's main building was used as a baggage receiving room and railroad ticketing office. Immigrants were required to set aside their bags—a nerve-wracking proposition—while they proceeded through processing. The experience is recalled in a dramatic exhibit (above). Inside often ragtag valises and bundles were religious articles, musical instruments, family jewelry, sentimental items, and household possessions (opposite) that sometimes represented everything that the immigrants owned.

Ellis Island's Registry Room (left) had the trappings of a cattle pen. The metal railings were later replaced with long benches. This photo was taken at a moment of relatively light traffic, for the room was sometimes jammed from wall to wall with newcomers. Those who reached this point had already passed an intrusive medical examination. One of the final stages was a check of paperwork (above), including one's job prospects in the New World.

Although the U.S. Coast Guard took over portions of Ellis Island in 1954, most spaces, including the main processing center exterior (above) and Registry Room (right), were allowed to deteriorate. Refurbished in the massive overhaul that included the Statue of Liberty, the Registry Room (overleaf) again shows off its vaulted Guastavino tile ceiling, installed in 1917—one year after a nearby munitions explosion, set by German agents, destroyed much of the building.

As part of the Registry Room renovation, distinctive chandeliers (above) were reconditioned. Along with the building's turreted towers, the processing center's arched windows (opposite) have become familiar symbols of Ellis Island. Off-Broadway actors—including, left to right, Gili Getz, Matthew Rankin, Margaret Flanagan, Andrew Mersmann, and Jim Maggard—portray immigrants and inspectors in a powerful on-site production. Visitors may also view a film documenting the Ellis experience and listen to the center's oral history collection.

Photographer Augustus Sherman captured
the images of many early Ellis Island immigrants
and their families—from dozens of countries.
Those above are Finns; the large and extended
family (right) are Scots. Sherman, or more likely
a bureaucrat, typed on the latter photo a
notation that this whole brood, having arrived
on the S.S. *Caledonia* in 1905, was welcomed
by a friend in Anniston, Alabama. These
photographs reflect the seriousness of purpose
that most immigrants possessed.

Accounts from the period make it clear that anyone who "looked funny" or acted abnormally at any point during the registration process was pulled from line and sent to another part of the complex for "mental testing" (above). However, immigration officials tried hard not to reject immigrants. Many inspectors were fluent in several languages, and other interpreters were brought in to help where needed. The fellow in colorful native garb (opposite) is identified only as "North African."

For immigrants from many cultures, medical testing was the most frightening and humiliating part of the Ellis Island routine. Exams (opposite) that came to be known as the "thirty-second medical" were uncomfortably public. Physicians were especially looking for any sign of contagious disease, as in eye exams (above) in which officials searched for any sign of a virulent infection called trachoma. Hospital, isolation, and quarantine wards were kept full of those who did not pass muster.

One of the detainees' hearing rooms (left) has been restored to how it looked circa 1911. About 10 percent of immigrants were held for legal hearings, especially if they were suspected of being "contract laborers" whose low wages could have threatened the pay structure of entrenched workers. Office gear used by the island's huge bureaucracy (above) was abandoned to dust and the elements when Ellis Island closed; but some was salvaged and is now on display.

Despite the crowded conditions and undercurrent of fear that pervaded Ellis Island, officials tried to humanize the registration experience. Children were given warm milk, and those who arrived late and had to stay overnight were fed meals (above) and housed in tight dormitory quarters—men in certain rooms, women and children in others. One of the dorm rooms (opposite) can be visited on the balcony level. There was even a rooftop play area (overleaf).

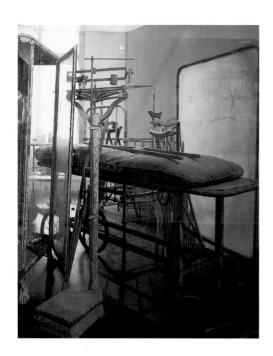

Hospital artifacts (above) from the period of abandonment have been placed on exhibit. They present a chilling testament to the conditions, and the uncertainties of acceptance, faced by new-comers who were pulled out of line for medical reasons. A children's ward (right) was one part of Ellis Island presenting the terrifying prospect of splitting apart families. Officials tried to let infectious diseases run their course in the compound hospital to avoid sending children home.

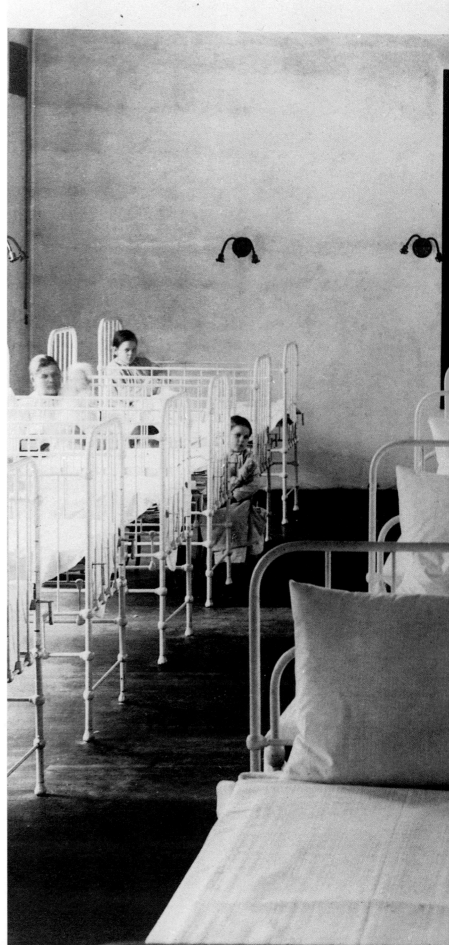

The facade of a hospital building (opposite) on Island Two betrays only a hint of the devastation within. Years of neglect, freezing and thawing and overheating, and deterioration (left) have left their mark. Grim reminders (above) of the nature of these facilities remain, however. In 1998 the U.S. Supreme Court awarded Islands Two and Three to New Jersey, and there has been talk of restoration and renewal. These photos illustrate the enormity of the challenge.

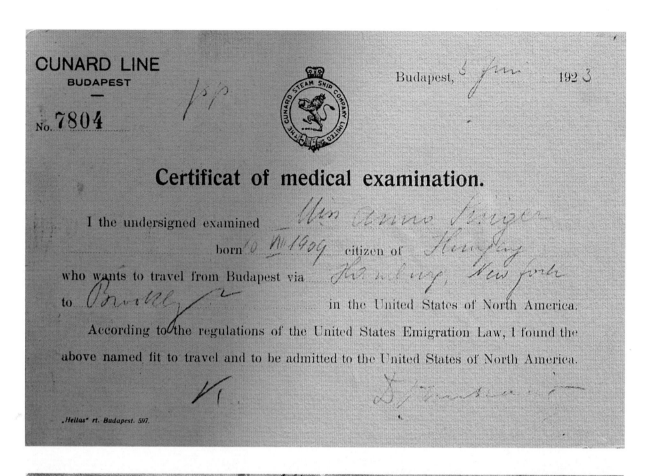

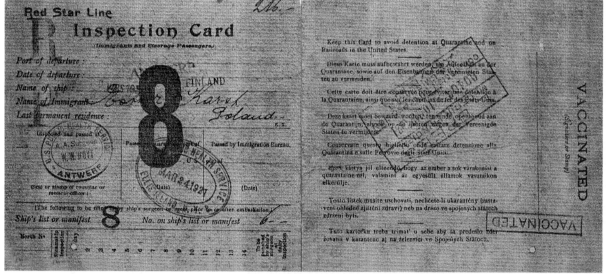

Paperwork, paperwork, paperwork! Ellis Island was an ordeal for immigrants, many of whom were illiterate, as they struggled to hold onto the proper medical certificates (top), inspection cards (bottom), and other documentation. One exhibit (opposite) shows the wide array of currency and coins handled by the money exchange. This was a private concession, and there were instances in which naive and unsuspecting immigrants were bilked of some or all of their life savings in this process.

One of the poignant places at Ellis Island is the "Stairs of Separation" (above), leading from the Registry Room. Immigrants trudged down them after processing—some to get train tickets (left), some to catch the ferry to Manhattan (overleaf), and an unfortunate few to head for detention or expulsion. However, despite Ellis's reputation as the "Isle of Tears," only about 2 percent of arriving immigrants were deported—half for medical and half for legal reasons.

The immediate destination for hundreds of thousands of Ellis Island arrivals was the teeming, squalid tenement district of Manhattan (left). Just as Irish immigrants crowded into apartment buildings in Boston, Italians and Jews, in particular, found refuge among their peers in burgeoning New York. Among the poor immigrants who entered the United States through Ellis Island and went on to fame, fortune, or both, were songwriter Irving Berlin (above), actress Claudette Colbert, aviation pioneer Igor Sikorsky, and Vaudeville singer Al Jolson. Most immigrants, though, quickly learned that America's streets were not "paved with gold."

WORKINGMEN!

WHICH DO YOU WANT?
AMERICAN OR EUROPEAN WAGES!

POTTERIES.

	English.	Trenton, N. J.
Plate makers,	$ 7 75	$20 40
Dish makers,	9 67	19 43
Cup makers,	9 97	18 50
Saucer makers,	7 97	18 50
Wash bowl makers,	9 71	25 64
Pressers,	8 18	17 12
Printers,	6 59	13 56
Kilnmen,	6 59	12 00
Saggur makers,	8 50	17 00
Mould makers,	10 29	20 00
Turners,	8 05	18 00
Handlers,	8 43	19 00

WINDOW GLASS.

	Ohio Valley Average, per Week.	Belgium Average, per W'k
Blowers,	$40 09	$20 00
Gatherers,	23 03	6 25
Flatners,	34 45	6 25
Cutters,	27 59	5 00

COAL MINERS AND COKE MAKERS.

TIME, TEN HOURS PER DAY.

Occupation.	W. Va. Wages, per Day	English Wages, per Day
Blacksmiths,	$2 00	$1 14
Blacksmiths' helpers.	1 25	72
Coal cleaner,	1 25	60
Drivers,	1 60	50
Engineers,	1 75	1 12
Furnacemen,	1 25	72
Laborers,	1 25	72
Miners,	1 40 to 1 87	1 12
Mine boss,	2 50	1 68
Track layer,	1 80	90
Trappers,	50	22
Weighers,	1 80	90

BLAST FURNACES.

	Ohio Valley per Day	Cumberland, Eng., per Day
Keepers,	$2 25	$1 41
Helpers,	1 65	85
Top fillers,	1 65	1 13
Bottom fillers,	1 65	1 13
Cinder loaders,	1 55	85
Blast engineer,	2 25	1 00
Cindermen,	1 65	1 11
General labor,	1 40	77

The wages of Blast Furnaces here denominated as Ohio Valley wages are the smallest west of the Allegheny Mountains. Those paid in Joliet, Ill., and even in Pittsburgh, are higher than those given here.

ROLLING MILL.

	West of Allegheny M'tn's, per Ton.	England, per Ton.
Puddling,	$5 50	$1 57
Muck rolling,	68¾	24
Bar rolling and catching,	1 13¾	73
Bar heating,	70	34
Hoop rolling and heating 1½" and No. 17,	3 50	1 80
Cotton tie rolling and heating,	4 10	2 37

BESSEMER STEEL WORKS.

	United States, per Day	England, per Day
Converter men,	$4 35, 12 h'rs.	$1 45
Steel works pit men,	4 00, 8 "	1 15 to 1 25
Steel works ladle men,	3 98, 12 "	1 00 to 1 15
Rail heaters,	5 00, 12 "	1 60
Rail rollers,	7 00, 12 "	2 50
Common laborers,	1 34, 10 "	62

(June, 1888.)

FLINT GLASS WORKERS.

	WEST VIRGINIA WAGES, PER DAY.	GREAT BRITAIN WAGES, PER DAY
Glass blowers, Pressers and Finishers,	$3 25 to 4 25	$ 96 to 1 20
First-class Castor place Workmen,	4 50 to 6 00	1 25 to 2 40
Punch Tumbler Blowers,	1 50 to 3 75	65 to 96

The hours of work in Europe are longer than in America for the same amount of work.

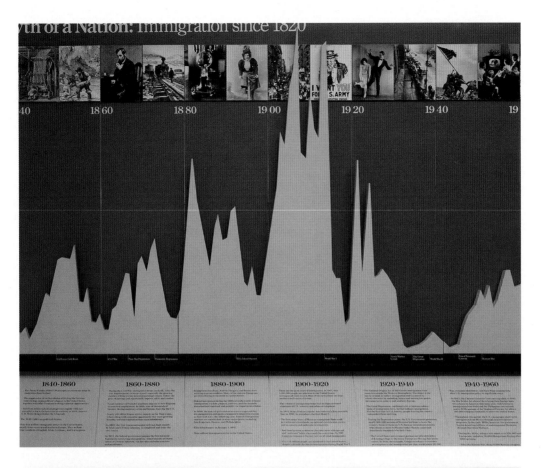

Unions, many of whose members were recent immigrants, published broadsides (opposite) warning about later arrivals' dire effect on wages. Ellis Island exhibits demonstrate the growing number of women immigrants (below left) and the peaks and valleys of immigration through the years (above left)—notably the decline after passage of the National Origins Act of 1924. More than five hundred thousand names have been etched on Ellis's Wall of Honor (overleaf) in remembrance of immigrants who passed through.

The very same Annie Moore who appears in
statuary on the wharf in Ireland's County Cork—
see page 1—can be found in the Ellis Island
Immigrant Museum. The first of twelve million
newcomers to pass through Ellis Island at age
eighteen, she received a hero's welcome and a
$10 gold piece. Annie married an Irishman,
moved to Texas, had eight children, and was
killed in a train wreck at age forty-six.